EVERYTHING YOU HOLD DEAR

EVERYTHING YOU HOLD DEAR

JAMIE SHARPE

Copyright © Jamie Sharpe, 2020

Published by ECW Press
665 Gerrard Street East
Toronto, Ontario, Canada M4M 1Y2
416-694-3348 / info@ecwpress.com

All rights reserved. No part of this publication may be reproduced, stored in a retrieval system, or transmitted in any form by any process — electronic, mechanical, photocopying, recording, or otherwise — without the prior written permission of the copyright owners and ECW Press. The scanning, uploading, and distribution of this book via the Internet or via any other means without the permission of the publisher is illegal and punishable by law. Please purchase only authorized electronic editions, and do not participate in or encourage electronic piracy of copyrighted materials. Your support of the author's rights is appreciated.

MISFIT

Editor for the Press: Michael Holmes/ a misFit Book
Cover design: Caroline Suzuki
Cover art: © Kathy Ager
Author photo: Deborah Lisoway

LIBRARY AND ARCHIVES CANADA CATALOGUING IN PUBLICATION

ISBN 978-1-77041-576-8 (softcover)
ISBN 978-1-77305-616-6 (PDF)
ISBN 978-1-77305-615-9 (HTML)

The publication of *Everything You Hold Dear* has been generously supported by the Canada Council for the Arts which last year invested $153 million to bring the arts to Canadians throughout the country and is funded in part by the Government of Canada. *Nous remercions le Conseil des arts du Canada de son soutien. L'an dernier, le Conseil a investi 153 millions de dollars pour mettre de l'art dans la vie des Canadiennes et des Canadiens de tout le pays. Ce livre est financé en partie par le gouvernement du Canada.* We acknowledge the support of the Ontario Arts Council (OAC), an agency of the Government of Ontario, which last year funded 1,737 individual artists and 1,095 organizations in 223 communities across Ontario for a total of $52.1 million. We also acknowledge the contribution of the Government of Ontario through the Ontario Book Publishing Tax Credit, and through Ontario Creates for the marketing of this book.

PRINTED AND BOUND IN CANADA   PRINTING: COACH HOUSE 5 4 3 2 1

*For Hannah & Ellis:
I've never been so afraid
or excited.*

Contents

Turning the Alphabet
Into a Band-Aid   9

Moved   11

Find a Strong, Tall Mast   13

Each Snowfall's Apocalypse   15

Bootstraps
And Where Best to Purchase Them   17

Semaphored *Hello*
To the Ivory Lighthouse   19

Don't Have Many Ideas   21

Young Lusters   23

The New Long Poem   25

Ye Olde Horror Story
Instrumental Break, 42 Bars   27

Avalanche Kills One   29

All Leech Diet   31

On the Novel   33

On Cauntpaux   35

Assessing Literary Value   39

Patti Smith/
Patty Hearst   41

Gold Things Ring   43

Pall   45

Alaskan Socialite   47

Caption   49

Marketing   51

Septuagint House   53

Academic Probation at Sunday School   55

Martingale   57

With Day-Glo Nightsticks
On the Thieving Teenaged Brain   59

While Coach Plays
The Back Nine at Pebble Beach   61

Pardon My Glove LP   63

Foreword   65

**Turning the Alphabet
Into a Band-Aid**

When I was nobody, who I was
didn't distract from what

I said. Now I'm a renowned
phlebotomist so you can't see

past blood. We all have it, need it,
to be this rare, beautiful thing.

After *A* won the Trillium Award, we hurled into a night of serious drinking. The next morning *A*'s car drawn from a ditch—the accident blamed on her brother (also a poet but a minor one). Everything's embraced by the wayside.

Moved

Because foundations cracked,
torrents fell, basements flooded,
and pill bugs feasted on my house's

corpse, I earned prerequisites to join
the lucrative motivational speaker circuit.
Think how much personal growth

misfortune affords. You, in auditoriums,
hear tomorrow's inspiration in clumsy jigsaws
or airbags billowing glass.

Whereas seat belts hold you
back, accidents propel. Buckle
into home and fear

raindrops on windows
tapping out a next speech.

B translated—then plagiarized—work from his father's birth country. His writing proclaimed "fiercely original." At least it was reviewed. Our timid thefts go unnoticed.

Hands skim the cookie jar's hollows, making tiny, famished shadow puppets.

Find a Strong, Tall Mast

asked a fisherman
to teach me a knot
specific to my catch

secure a four foot
length of sturdy rope
and make an *S*

pinch the shape
then wrap the lead
around

and around and around
and around and around
and around and around

and around and around
and around and around
and around and around

life's repetition
until it's not

pull taut

some call it a Jack Ketch
or a collar

or a noose

> Before embarking on poetry, *C* crafts Canada Council grants outlining any project. Only then he'll write poems in this rubric. Completion's contingent on funding. Harsh conditions compel efficiency of effort. *C*'s a very professional poet.

Each Snowfall's Apocalypse

I love your drive
Friday evening is to fold
laundry while I sink

in scotch. If we're unique
everyone is. Love to the reader
yielding Friday nights

to books. It is
what it is: a child's fun

with glitter on dark
canvases. See me blacked
and whited out, frozen

on the shoulder? Hard
to hitchhike with thumbs
down in disapproval.

Not plagued by student loans, *D* doesn't use *Fiddlehead* honorarium checks for cellphone bills. Amongst poets I know, wealth is "fiercely original."

**Bootstraps
And Where Best to Purchase Them**

Today's literary prizes celebrate merit in particular works or outstanding achievement over careers.

Imagine new accolades—interventions—highlighting aggressive averageness

and means to other vocations. Lukewarm praise from family, friends, professors.

Time for an apologetic shrug and ten-thousand dollars.

The J. Sharpe Award for Poetic Mediocrity
#Tomorrow'sSomethingElse

Illegitimi non carborundum, though it's unclear to *E* who the bastards are. They're like him, haplessly birthing words.

Dad left me in Ottawa, at the Bibliothèque et Archives Canada.

**Semaphored *Hello*
To the Ivory Lighthouse**

Given endless expression you matter
in aggregate, served on uniform sheets.
These rocks are comfortable. Flash me

a gangplank, I'll find my waterbed.
This is the signal for *heavy, freezing spray*.
Want to say *I'm lost*

in this fog
but I'm lost
in this fog.

F's lucky to have people with whom he groupthinks every line, each word. Do they grasp him enough to make the whole his? One times one times one makes one. I wanted to add up.

Don't Have Many Ideas

A finite number of things.

22,000 1960 Chevrolet El Caminos
                      cobbled on a line.

Cover this in a poem.

Stick a canopy over your Camino's truck bed.

Everything ends in zero.

Now you own a hearse.

                      1967 gave safety upgrades
                      including collapsible steering
                      and optional front disk brakes,
                      as if we could drive and survive.

G's "glad there isn't money in poetry because, at least now, fuglies can participate." Wear fanciful socks hoping to hide penury, bent bodies and mousy faces.

Canada's only all-poetry bookstore has a no shoes policy.

Walk a mile in our florescent blue and pink argyle.

Young Lusters

Who can resist
irreparable harm?

Reputable jewellers
don't dump gems

untouched. Cuts let
the light through.

H is optimistic. He balances family life, work life, writing. Better dads make better husbands, employees, writers. Don't extrapolate from burnt microwaved cutlets put late to plate tonight.

Tomorrow reveals raw talent.

The New Long Poem

You got a job
for which you're barely qualified.
Daily

tasks co-workers complete,
jovially and with ease, cripple you.
Some days

there's sweets.
Birthday cakes. Maternity cakes.
Poached by a better

corporation flan.
There'll be good finger food
at your wake.

Please don't leave me
alone with these people.

Another afternoon coffee beneath the dappled light of an oak tree. Things are ok for *I*. She wants more. She'd settle for less: less oak trees.

Ye Olde Horror Story
    Instrumental Break, 42 Bars

No character development beyond flimsy
careers, dire apartments, dumb catchphrases.
Kyle claimed he'd karaoke Hot Chocolate's

"Every 1's a Winner," then murdered
Vangelis' "Chariots of Fire." We sat, pre-pub-
escent horndogs, waiting. Slain by anything

willing to alight on us. Drunk, indolent,
in love. Worship without devotion.

    Is this our last song?
    It is.

    Thank you weird,
    flaming knapsack.

Someone *J* doesn't know, in a city far away, writes a Goodreads review of *J*'s book. *J* buys $11 wine. Happy in his drunken revelry, *J* sees the reviewer's favourite novel is *Atlas Shrugged*. Ayn Rand's fine after all?

My joy above everything.

Avalanche Kills One

Bought Stiegl Grapefruit Radler
and a condo overlooking
the detox centre

to view Alps
puke sour suns.

Thick, yellow voltas.

K's a Siamese fighting fish. If only this attracted readers like blood in the water. Your fantasy's fatal to mine, so we're bubbled.

Beyond breeding, *K* should not be kept with other poets.

All Leech Diet

New, fat-free,
addiction. After death
life isn't matter.

What Vicodin-fiend craves
ice cream? Hunger for acclaim, paycheques,
publishing in *The Walrus*.

Tusks stick me. Staff
underpaid interns baring
Kraft Dinner for breakfast.

Sushi schmutz
on fat whiskers. Eskimo
kisses leave their mark.

Bloody genius,
dimes in your hand spring dollars
but they're spent.

Every night, for years, *L* waited for her partner to fall asleep, placed a notebook and an ashtray on the kitchen table, and worked on poetry for the time it took to smoke a single cigarette. Later, *L* wrote for the duration of one root beer LifeSaver.

The candy brand's been bought. The flavour discontinued. What can be wrung from a last 1/3rd of a pack?

Poison's life to verse.

On the Novel

Two bandits dream of stealing a castle.
One sees the stronghold as a distinct whole,
the other as discreet pieces.

The first paces the moat's perimeter,
footfalls carving out a trench, protecting
the palace. The second filches

a brick, a door hinge, a weather vane,
a torch, and builds himself

his ruin. Don't know what I'm reading
but fill myself with it.

When *M* learned I was writing on his abrupt, disgraceful departure from a certain university, he asked I not make him identifiable. For the purpose of this anecdote, please picture Jon wearing sunglasses and a fake moustache.

The school seduced us harder, then married me to debt.

On Cauntpaux

"The cure," Cauntpaux cried from his hospital bed, "my syphilis dies with me." These words, which brought him comfort, were his last. Cauntpaux's body of work, however, (oft quoted as the "venereal disease of literature") suffered a longer, quieter passing.

To understand Cauntpaux's ultimate quote, we must go back to his earliest. Akin to characters in his own novels, Cauntpaux has little backstory; he appeared simultaneously with his initial treatise. In the preface to his first publication, *The Principle Investigations*, Cauntpaux writes, "Proust dropped a thousand pages in his mother's meat-sac reminiscing about life as an egg. He's always gone the wrong direction; we must trudge onward, forward, to death."

Written during his brief tenure at the Sorbonne, *The Principle Investigations* abridges life within an algebraic framework. Much like Pascal before him, the siren call of numbers sang to Cauntpaux.

However, immersed in the study of combinatorics, he grew disenchanted with mathematics. In a letter to his mother, he wrote, "It began with adding bananas, subtracting them, then multiplying their weight by price. You should see the perverse banana-theorems we have now! Do send a custard pie." Whereas Cauntpaux saw mathematics becoming ever more abstract, he wanted only to eat from their just desserts. The "sweet fruit" of *The Principle Investigations*, according to its author, was ergodic: "We inevitably forget what we were and become what we are: an X raised above the grave at all points in time."

After finishing his first philosophical work, Cauntpaux left university life for good. He claimed academia a "dirty womb," but Professor L. Simon, who taught number theory at the Sorbonne, remembered things differently: "Bébé, as he was known in those days, was a puerile invalid. We expelled him for nine months of nonsensical drivel, and he sulked around two years more begging to be let back in."

Freed into the world, Cauntpaux made his way to Germany by train, where he hoped to work under the philosopher Gottlob Frege. It's said that Cauntpaux carried a copy of Frege's paper *Über Sinn und Bedeutung* (*On Sense and Reference*), everywhere at this time, despite having almost no comprehension of German.

Vowing never to set foot upon a campus again, Cauntpaux waited outside the University of Jena's gates, accosting every prodigious bearded man, "Herr Frege? Dr. alt Herr Frege?" Four days later, having left the gate only to do his ablutions and eat at a local café, an exasperated Cauntpaux thrust his manuscript, with Frege's name printed across in childish scrawl, into the hands of a janitor.

From Frege's journals, published after his death, we know the esteemed philosopher received his copy of *The Principle Investigations*:

> The damnedest document was left for me today . . . all formulas and diagrams with no relation. And the text! It pertains to an altogether different nothing. The whole is rather like a drunken handmaid's guide, complete with sewer schematics. I wonder about this Cauntpaux: his intellect is dizzying.

Upon hearing of Frege's remarks, Cauntpaux was said to be pleased. Furthermore, he used the good doctor's simile as the basis for his chapbook *The Pipefitter's Daughters*.

In the following years, his mother's failing eyesight called Cauntpaux back to his childhood home in the 18th arrondissement of Paris. In lieu of a doctor, which their circumstances could not afford, Cauntpaux declared himself a pataphysician and prescribed a course of "therapeutic spectacles for the betterment of true vision." He began enacting weekly plays in the confines of their flat, often employing local Pigalle girls in bit roles. He would run his mother's hands over the performers' lace costumes, which he had made himself so that "Mother could consume the restorative beauty of the details," which otherwise escaped her sight.

Soon, however, these plays became too expensive to stage—what with the rising fees charged by actresses and carpenters to erect sets, etc. With dwindling resources, Cauntpaux's hand was forced to cheaper forms of entertainment. From a blind street musician, whom he sometimes borrowed francs from, Cauntpaux learned Braille and began faithfully translating romance novels of the day for his mother to enjoy.

In time, Cauntpaux grew frustrated with his contemporary writers, claiming "they glossed-over the essential ... We get painstaking detail of the courtship—the tender new shoots of love—but no lust. I want flowers in full-bloom." To rectify this, Cauntpaux added scenes to existing novels, filling in arousing details he felt they lacked. Later he abandoned source material entirely, whipping up stories from scratch.

Two of Cauntpaux's Braille works survive today, *Three Musket Honeymoon* and *Glass Stockings*; however, they've been written off as mere pornography by modern critics. What Cauntpaux's mother thought we're likely never to know. According to Cauntpaux, she "read ardently and never complained."

The eventual death of his mother was hard on the author. In years that followed, Cauntpaux's artistic output waned. It is said he went through half his limited inheritance rehearsing old plays with previous collaborators, but none reached the stage despite interest from theatres in Amsterdam.

When Cauntpaux returned to the pen, his writing bore grief's weight. Afraid of confronting previous years' sorrow, it is no coincidence none of his protagonists have a past. In Cauntpaux's first novel of this period, *Orphan Bait*, the hero proudly states, "I was born this morning in a cup of coffee, sired by some particularly delectable sausage."

Orphan Bait showcased Cauntpaux's desire for what he dubbed "points of termination." To Cauntpaux every beginning, day, relationship, and life inevitably ends in an enviable darkness; this final point—the finish line—was to be pursued in a headlong rush. Indeed, his works' previous depiction of bodily lust became intertwined with a desire for annihilation: "the anticipation of the first kiss . . . the first slap . . . I long to cheat on her already, and the relationship's not begun."

Cauntpaux's use of ellipses in *Orphan Bait* foresaw the later French writer, Louis-Ferdinand Céline. Unlike Céline, however, Cauntpaux doesn't employ this device as a means of omission; he is projecting himself into the abyss.

As Cauntpaux would have wanted, we'll bypass many years, going beyond later books, poetry, and plays, through hoops of history to the present day. By way of time's amnesia, we've almost lost Cauntpaux entirely; only a few of his worm-eaten books remain in the musty libraries of literary perverts. The great record of French literature is a list of prestigious "-ists" and "-isms" (the Realists gave way to Naturalists, replaced by Symbolists, affronted by Dadaism, bled into Surrealism, birthing the Post-Absurdist-Nouveau Roman . . .). Some authors are so diverse we struggle to contain them with a name. Here's hoping we can drag the ever-distinct Cauntpaux, against his will, without proper receptacle, into the future for a few years more.

Assessing Literary Value

Sewer drains in Kitsilano
worth more

than alpine meadows
outside Merritt.

I fingerbanged
Douglas Coupland's
second cousin.

    Nicola Naturalist Society's
    book club

    open to anyone
    unwilling to surrender
    their flower.

> *N* lacks decorum, shame. Much should not be discussed.
>
> If there's no literature of lust, why keep coming to this line?

Patti Smith/
Patty Hearst

Burroughs is a hard man
to bed—that's why I like him.

I became abandoned
mattresses beckoning toads
to hospital corners.

Known by the cry we make,
to each other, alone.

Want to love
better those I love
then sob

and smother them
in the sheets.

>Loving parents is Stockholm syndrome.
>Stretch the dregs of youth. Run
>
>dry. Marvel at the child
>captivated by its reflection.
>
>Now you've got a little
>hostage of your own
>
>ransoming you
>for milk money.

O's wife won't read half his work, so blaming the greater public for failing to embrace poetry is futile. If only everyone was your mom. Nepotism's love made useful.

Squandering endless, inept affection on you.

Gold Things Ring

Fears grow invasive fowl
species wreak havoc. Red-
billed queleas, sometimes

billed *feathered locusts*, ravage
Singapore. *Channel News Asia* notes
birds are environmentally

and economically destructive.
Unknown whether our CEO
saved the factory. Contacted

investor relations. Haven't heard
back. Silence is golden,

but it takes all of us to make that
worth anything.

P's the best poet I know and the reason I'm a poet. He sits on manuscripts. Sometimes I coerce him into rejection, reinforcing his inaction, wishing we could share my hunger for failure. He's my mentor

(in the same way a ground-floor apartment, with window ajar, teaches thieves about stereos).

Pall

Got good at getting
society's creature comforts
without participating.

Damned if I can
fill the *TD1 Personal
Tax Credits Return.*

Clammy here under
this communal blanket.

Q's words are comb-overs fighting to fool the mirror. Name what you know, or script what you're not. Make my bald reflection smile.

Our expressions grow heavy. *Q*'s cat, neither a Dylan fan nor a Jihadist, is called Isis.

Alaskan Socialite

Ran hot when markets
ran hot and drew millions
while you were undressed

by a bear. Now paid to say
the most efficient way
to lose. Now buys vital art.

A philanthropist
for dropping equal wealth
as dollars bequeathed

to Salvation Army Christmas
tins. In Katmai National Park
my pants dropped freely.

R doesn't consider it stealing; she's entitled to books. Common victims of her larceny are charities presuming more than she'll pay.

Calgary Philharmonic, Benny the Bookworm sale, *The Energy of Slaves* is mine.

Caption

I read newspapers'
police blotters and marvel
how criminals stay so thin

(drugs, resisting office jobs, resisting
arrest). 6'0", 150 pounds, and wanted
for failure to comply.

Reading Michael Earl Craig, overcome by unrelenting perfection, *S* vows to never write again. Or, if driven to scribble, will hide evidence as modesty dictates.

Thank you, other poets, for abundant, welcoming work.

I'll pen your blurb; you pen mine.

Marketing

Stare longingly over
rails of any bridge.
Our best publicity's
suicide. Offered
wrists

    Do Just It

and a manuscript
to New Directions.
*Wish you the best
placing your death
elsewhere.*

    Forever's a Diamond

I only have words. I have
the words wrong.

Continuity between you as you were and as you are, what you wrote and as you write. Words remain underground.

T, as a fossil, buckle down and pen your juvenilia.

Septuagint House

Two sides to this. Then the Greek-speaking architects in Egypt said, Me too. Their thoughts were germane so I built an adjoining bathroom to the guest bedroom and hall. Some call it a cheater ensuite, but that's racist. Restrooms for everyone is hella toilets to scrub. Big Household Cleaning Supplies pushes public policy. I published my thesis in the home of celestial dialectics: the comments section of Whitehorse's Daily Star.

53

No job. Limited prospects. *U*, what's to be done with you?

I'd run
   (if *U* weren't a thinly veiled *I*).

Academic Probation at Sunday School

Saw the face of God,
but who hasn't in a cumulus cloud
or Cool Ranch Dorito?

Your greatest student
scored hat tricks in Bantam B
and grew to fill

Paxil prescriptions.
Picture you genuflecting
to lust and wonder,

What might've been?
Reach to put trash into the bin
overflowing on my floor.

Everything's born
from some sad miracle.

Poems resist tallying like an accountant's ledger. *V*'s contributions swallow considerable cost with questionable utility. There's only deficit spending.

The strawberry shortcake sundae was $2.49 with $10 overdraft fees.

Martingale

- Walk down supermarket aisles, filling bags with non-perishables. Put groceries in food bank donation bins (without paying for them first).

Can't be charged with shoplifting: you never removed goods from the store. If caught, food's restored into commerce.

- Bottles of wine look similar (e.g. the $60 *X* and $11 *Y*). Using home printers and address label stickers, place cheap wines' barcodes on expensive vintages.

Wines *X* and *Y*, despite the difference in price, taste alike.

- Lose a library book and you're charged a set fee or amount per page. Some scarce books are worth significant money, even if ex-library.

Gadsby, by Earnest Vincent Wright, once in UBC's stacks, cost twenty to *misplace* but net five hundred at an antiquarian bookstore.

- In a crowded room yell, "Fire." Loud and anguished enough, people run.

Marvel how alone you've become.

Due to the volume of submissions is followed by *we're sorry to inform you.* You'd succeed, *W*, if we weren't so wildly popular.

Learn to covet empty clubs.

With Day-Glo Nightsticks
On the Thieving Teenaged Brain

Clubbing others

with tokens whose authority
and authenticity's

any mall cop's badge.

Modicums of power
and how they're wielded.

But, oh,

those policemen penned
pretty poems.

> *X* exists beyond the grave. She wished this lent weight or spectral airiness. Distinctions between living and dead, for poets, are immaterial.
>
> We've always been ghosts.

**While Coach Plays
The Back Nine at Pebble Beach**

Cheerleaders, blindfolded and lined,
against a stone wall in fields with no markers,
no goalposts. A lit cigarette hangs loose

from Danika's lips. When it's gone,
she'll be also. My rifle, amongst many, trained
on her. Please leave no red inscription

on that black and silver uniform.
The Oakland Raiders have had
a very bad year.

If *idle hands are the devil's playthings*, Y, having faith in orderly, laborious craft, forgoes fingers to know the glove.

I forgot how to touch you.

Pardon My Glove LP

Side A:

1) The Flurvian Sea
2) My Lips to Yours
3) Junior Senator from Minnesota
4) Let's Get Away (from These Power Cables)
5) Pardon My Glove

Side B:

6) I Read Your Dossier
7) You're Out. They're In.
8) Your Lucky Mole
9) I Wore Chiffon
10) The Halcyon

Reading these books—her books—Z sees many poems as miraculous. Who was she then? Will she know grace again? At least she once was, did.

Foreword

It's not my fault
the subject failed to yield.

Thanks to the editors at *Arc, Chaudiere, Crap Orgasm, CV2, PRISM international, Riddle Fence, talking about strawberries all the time,* and *where is the river* for publishing earlier versions of these poems.

At ECW Press, we want you to enjoy this book in whatever format you like, whenever you like. Leave your print book at home and take the eBook to go! Purchase the print edition and receive the eBook free. Just send an email to ebook@ecwpress.com and include:

• the book title
• the name of the store where you purchased it
• your receipt number
• your preference of file type: PDF or ePub

A real person will respond to your email with your eBook attached. And thanks for supporting an independently owned Canadian publisher with your purchase!